CCSS Genre Real

M000106855

Essential Que...
How are kids around the world different?

A NEW LIFE IN INDIA

by Christopher Herrera
illustrated by Laura Freeman

Chapter 1
Getting to Know India 2

Chapter 2
Going to School 7

Chapter 3
After-school Activities II

Chapter 4
School Spirit Day I3

Respond to Reading I6

PAIRED READ Dress Around the World I7

Focus on Literary Elements 20

Getting to Know India

Mason Jones and his family are moving to India. They drive from the airport to their new home. Mason is surrounded by interesting sights. "Look at this traffic!" he exclaims.

rickshaw

Mr. and Mrs. Jones have friends in India. The Guptas have two sons. Raj is in fifth grade. Dev is Mason's age. They will be in second grade together.

Mason has heard about a special day at school called School Spirit Day. He can't wait to ask Dev about it!

sari

3

The two families go to a cricket match. Cricket is India's favorite sport. Dev and Mason watch the players run.

"Mason, I think you will love cricket! It is like baseball. Two teams play," Dev explains. "One team bats while the other team fields. When a player hits a ball, he runs between two areas like bases. If a person catches the ball, the batter is out. The teams change places after 10 outs."

> **In Other Words**   tries to catch the ball. En español: *trata de atrapar la pelota.*

batter

The families have dinner after the cricket match. Mrs. Gupta made lamb curry. She also made a spinach dish and roti. Roti is a warm, flat bread.

Mason's plate is filled with food. "Mrs. Gupta, this is delicious!" he exclaims. "It is spicy. I taste many different flavors!"

roti

saag paneer

paneer

STOP AND CHECK

What has Mason learned about India?

6

CHAPTER 2

Going to School

The next day, Mason walks to the Guptas' house. He wears a white uniform. Raj and Dev wear the same uniform. The three boys go to the same school.

uniforms

Mason and Dev study math, English, and science. Then they eat lunch. Dev describes School Spirit Day.

"I can't wait for School Spirit Day tomorrow! Our class will <u>do</u> a play. We also eat special snacks. At the end of the day, they give out awards!"

"It sounds fun! I hope I get to be in the play!" Mason says.

cafeteria

8

In social studies class, the boys learn about India's Independence Day. India celebrates its independence on August 15.

Dev explains how his family celebrates the holiday. "We go to a parade and eat sweets. Then we have a picnic. At night, there are fireworks! They look like colorful flowers. Maybe this year you can celebrate with us, Mason!"

flag

Mason tells the class about America's Independence Day. "America celebrates its independence on July 4. We have parades and picnics, too. We also have fireworks at night!"

STOP AND CHECK

What subjects has Mason studied that day?

CHAPTER 3
After-school Activities

Dev has a music lesson after school. Mason travels with him. Dev is learning to play the tabla. It is a type of drum. Dev shows Mason how to play it. "I use my fingers and palms to play. I play one drum with my right hand and the other with my left. Here, you try, Mason!"

tabla

Then the boys go to see Raj. Raj is practicing an Indian dance with other children. They wear colorful costumes. They form circles that move in different directions. The dancers hit colorful sticks together to the beat of the music.

STOP AND CHECK

What has Mason learned about Indian music and dance?

sticks

12

CHAPTER 4

School Spirit Day

School Spirit Day has arrived! Everyone is excited. Mason's class is performing a play. Dev and Mason both get parts. They wonder what else their class will <u>come up with</u>.

"I can't wait to be in a play! I am excited to wear a costume!" Mason says.

> **In Other Words**   think of. En español: *se les ocurrirá.*

stage

Some children will get awards. Children can get awards for doing well in school or sports.

"Maybe we will both get an award!" says Dev.

Language Detective	Quotation marks (" ") are used to show dialogue. Find another set of quotation marks on page 13.

award

Mason loves his new home! He has great new friends. He has a new school. He has fun new customs. "I love it here! I feel like the luckiest kid in the world!" Mason exclaims.

STOP AND CHECK

What Indian customs does Mason enjoy?

15

Respond to Reading

Summarize

Use important details to summarize *A New Life in India.*

	India	U.S.
holiday		
custom		

Text Evidence

1. How do you know *A New Life in India* is realistic fiction? Genre

2. How are Mason and Dev alike and different? Use story details to support your answer. Compare and Contrast

3. Use what you know about similes to find a simile for fireworks on page 9. Similes

4. Write about Mason's new home. Use details to tell what it is like.

Write About Reading

Compare Texts
Read about clothing customs around the world.

Dress Around the World

Some women in India wear saris. A sari is a long strip of cloth. This cloth is wrapped around the body. It is common to wrap the sari over the shoulder.

Saris are made of wide rectangles of cloth, often with colorful patterns.

sari

17

Some women and men in Japan wear kimonos. They usually wear them for special occasions.

A kimono is a long robe. It has a square shape. It has a sash called an *obi*.

Kimonos are often made of silk.

obi

Kanga is a long piece of colorful cloth. Women in eastern Africa wear it. Some men do, too. It is wrapped around the body in different ways.

The kanga has a different design in the center.

kanga

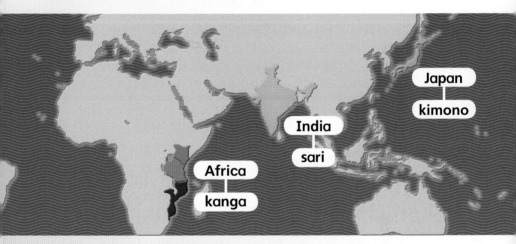

Japan

kimono

India

sari

Africa

kanga

 Make Connections

What do you think kids around the world wear? Essential Question

Look at both selections. What have you learned about India? Text to Text

Focus on
Literary Elements

Characters Characters are the people or animals in a story.

What to Look for You learn about characters from what they say and do. Illustrations help you learn about characters, too. Dev and Mason are characters in *A New Life in India*. You learn about them from what they say and do.

Your Turn

Think of two characters living in another country. Think about what they both are like. Plan a short story about them. Plan what they will say and do. Then write your story. Show how the two characters are alike and different.